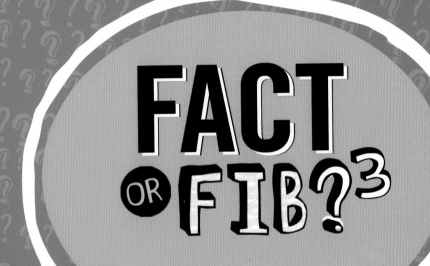

FACT OR FIB?³

D1056445

FACT
OR FIB? 3

A CHALLENGING GAME OF TRUE OR FALSE

KATHY FURGANG

STERLING CHILDREN'S BOOKS
New York

STERLING CHILDREN'S BOOKS
New York

An Imprint of Sterling Publishing
1166 Avenue of the Americas
New York, NY 10036

STERLING CHILDREN'S BOOKS and the distinctive Sterling Children's Books logo are trademarks of Sterling Publishing Co., Inc.

© 2015 by Sterling Publishing Co., Inc.
All rights reserved. No part of this publication may be reproduced, stored in a retrieval system, or transmitted in any form or by any means (including electronic, mechanical, photocopying, recording, or otherwise) without prior written permission from the publisher.

ISBN 978-1-4549-1588-1

Distributed in Canada by Sterling Publishing
c/o Canadian Manda Group, 664 Annette Street
Toronto, Ontario, Canada M6S 2C8. Distributed in the United Kingdom by GMC Distribution Services
Castle Place, 166 High Street, Lewes, East Sussex, England BN7 1XU
Distributed in Australia by Capricorn Link (Australia) Pty. Ltd.
P.O. Box 704, Windsor, NSW 2756, Australia

For information about custom editions, special sales, and premium and corporate purchases, please contact
Sterling Special Sales at 800-805-5489 or specialsales@sterlingpublishing.com.

Manufactured in China
Lot #:
2 4 6 8 10 9 7 5 3 1
08/15

www.sterlingpublishing.com/kids

How much do you really know about the world around you? Can you tell a fun fact from a wacky fib? **FACT** or **FIB?**[3] gives you tons of chances to test your knowledge of sports, fitness, and health. Here's how to play. The pages in this book are presented in sets of four. First, read the three statements on the pair of pages stamped **FACT or FIB?**. Guess which two of these statements are totally true—and which one is a whacky whopper. Then turn the page to check your answers and get more interesting information about each statement.

Test your friends, your parents, or even your teacher! Then give them those little nuggets of knowledge that reveal the correct answer. They're sure to be surprised!

A BASKETBALL RIM IS TWICE THE DIAMETER OF A BASKETBALL.

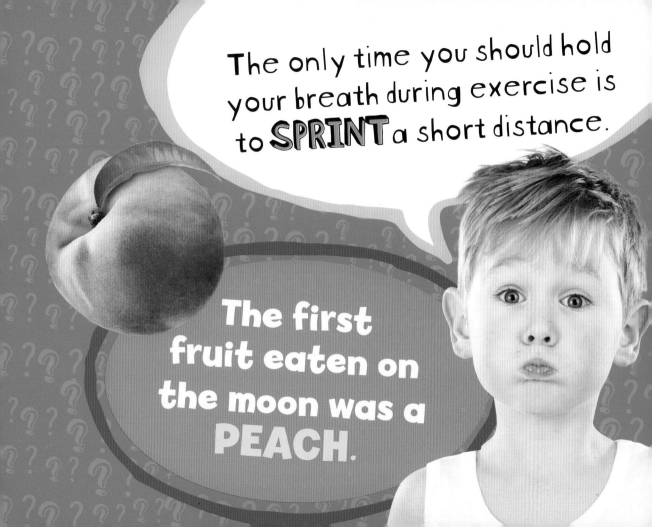

FACT

AN NBA BASKETBALL IS
9 INCHES (22.9 CM) ACROSS,
AND THE RIM IS 18 INCHES
(ABOUT 45.7 CM) ACROSS.
THE HOOP IS EXACTLY 10 FEET
(3 M) OFF THE FLOOR.

FIB

The only time you should hold your breath while exercising is while **SWIMMING UNDER WATER**.

FACT

The first meal that APOLLO 11 astronauts had on the moon was bacon, canned peaches, sugar cookies, coffee, and juice.

An Olympic gold medal is made of **SOLID GOLD**.

The **HUMAN HEART** weighs about as much as a softball.

A BEAN BURRITO HAS AS MUCH PROTEIN AS A SERVING OF CHICKEN.

FIB

Gold medals from the Olympics are made of about 99% SILVER. Just the outside covering, about 1%, is gold. This makes the medals much lighter and cheaper to make than if they were made of solid gold.

FACT

The heart is about the SIZE OF A FIST and the WEIGHT OF A SOFTBALL. Your heart pumps blood all around your body.

A 3-OUNCE (85 G) SERVING OF CHICKEN HAS ABOUT **21 GRAMS OF PROTEIN.** PROTEIN IS IN EVERY CELL OF YOUR BODY AND HELPS KEEP BONES, MUSCLES, SKIN, AND BLOOD HEALTHY.

FACT OR FIB?

The length of a marathon is **26.2 MILES** (42.2 km).

The human body has
FIVE
types of
MUSCLES.

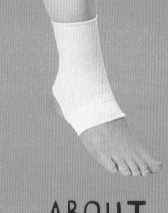

ABOUT
28,000
AMERICANS
SPRAIN AN
ANKLE
EACH DAY.

FACT

The length of a marathon was set up for the 1908 London Olympics as **26 miles** (41.8 km). The extra **352 yards** (321.9 m) were added so the race would end in front of the royal family's viewing box.

FIB The body has three types of muscles. **"SMOOTH"** muscles work without you even thinking about them, for swallowing or digesting food. **"SKELETAL"** muscles cover your bones. And **"CARDIAC"** muscles are found only in your heart.

ANKLE SPRAINS MAKE UP ALMOST HALF OF ALL SPORTS INJURIES. IT CAN TAKE UP TO SIX WEEKS FOR A SPRAINED ANKLE TO HEAL.

FACT

FACT OR **FIB?**

The average person walks about **70,000** miles (112,654.1 km) during a lifetime.

The fastest tennis serve ever recorded was 130 miles (209.2 km) per hour.

FACT

All of the walking an average person does in a lifetime, including to school, to the kitchen, or to the bathroom, REALLY ADDS UP! 70,000 miles is the same distance as three trips around Earth's equator.

FIB

Australian tennis player SAMUEL GROTH set a new record in 2012 when he hit a serve at 163 miles (263 km) per hour. Despite the superfast serve, he lost this match to Uladzimir Ignatik from Belarus.

THE COMMON COLD CAN BE CAUSED BY MORE THAN 200 DIFFERENT VIRUSES. IT IS RESPONSIBLE FOR BILLIONS OF DOLLARS IN MEDICAL COSTS EACH YEAR.

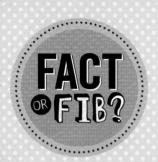

FACT OR **FIB?**

Up to 85% of skiing injuries are caused by falls.

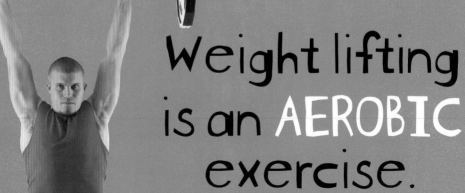

Weight lifting is an AEROBIC exercise.

EATING A BANANA CAN HELP LOWER YOUR TEMPERATURE.

FACT

Most ski injuries are caused by falls. About 10% of ski injuries involve hitting objects or other skiers, and about 5% happen because of accidents on ski lifts.

FIB

Aerobic exercise brings up the heart rate because of an increase in oxygen use. Weight lifting is called ANAEROBIC EXERCISE. Anaerobic exercise builds muscle.

FACT

TRY EATING A BANANA ON A HOT DAY OR WHEN YOU HAVE A FEVER. THEY HAVE BEEN SHOWN TO SLIGHTLY LOWER THE BODY'S TEMPERATURE.

25

FACT OR **FIB?**

ABOUT 30% OF ELEMENTARY SCHOOL STUDENTS BUY SCHOOL LUNCH ON ANY GIVEN DAY.

Exercise can help the body age **MORE SLOWLY**.

An astronaut played golf on the moon.

ABOUT 60% OF ELEMENTARY SCHOOL STUDENTS BUY LUNCH. THAT NUMBER DECREASES WITH AGE. ABOUT 54% OF MIDDLE SCHOOL STUDENTS BUY LUNCH AND ABOUT 44% OF HIGH SCHOOL STUDENTS BUY LUNCH EACH DAY.

FIB

FACT After the age of 40, bones and muscles naturally become weaker. Exercise is needed to keep bones and muscles strong.

FACT In 1971, astronaut Alan Shepard hit two golf balls on the moon. One of them flew far into the distance because the moon's gravity is 83.3% less than Earth's. The ball is still on the moon today!

BURNS, BATTER, BALTIMORE.

Printed baseball cards have been around since the **1860s**.

THE PILGRIMS AT PLYMOUTH ROCK FOUND NATIVE AMERICANS PLAYING A FORM OF SOCCER.

FACT

In the 1860s, a sporting goods company began printing cards with a team picture on one side and an advertisement on the other. They were the first baseball cards.

THE PILGRIMS WHO LANDED IN MASSACHUSETTS IN 1620 REPORTED THAT NATIVES ALONG THE COAST PLAYED A GAME THEY CALLED PASUCKQUAKKOHOWOG, OR "THEY GATHER TO PLAY FOOTBALL."

FACT

Only **SIX STATES** require physical education every school day in grades K-12. In **ILLINOIS**, **HAWAII**, **MASSACHUSETTS**, **MISSISSIPPI**, **NEW YORK**, and **VERMONT**, you can bet kids will get some exercise every day.

The first Olympic Games in Athens, Greece, had **22 female ATHLETES**.

OLYMPIAD

34

A plate of **COLORFUL FOODS** has more nutrients than a plate of **DULL-COLORED FOODS.**

WALKING A **DOG** IS CONSIDERED REGULAR EXERCISE.

FIB

The first Olympic games, in 1896, featured **311 MALE ATHLETES**, but **NO FEMALE ATHLETES**. There were 22 female athletes in the 1900 Paris Games, when women competed for the first time.

FACT Different colors in fruits and vegetables, such as **RED**, **ORANGE**, **BLUE**, and **GREEN**, mean that the foods have certain vitamins and minerals. The more colorful the plate, the more nutrients you will be eating!

FACT JUST GETTING OUT THERE AND MOVING IS AN EXAMPLE OF EXERCISE. WALK A DOG, TAKE SOME STAIRS, OR RIDE A BIKE. IT ALL COUNTS!

FACT OR FIB?

MARATHONS TAKE PLACE ONLY IN THE UNITED STATES.

Exercise releases CHEMICALS into the body that make you FEEL GOOD.

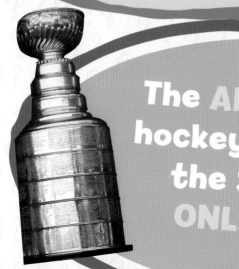

The ANAHEIM DUCKS hockey team has won the Stanley Cup ONLY ONE TIME.

EVERY YEAR, THERE ARE MORE THAN 500 MARATHONS IN 64 COUNTRIES AROUND THE WORLD.

FIB

FACT Chemicals called ENDORPHINS are released into the body during exercise, and the body's emotions are controlled by these quick chemical messages.

FACT The ANAHEIM DUCKS are part of the Western Conference of the NATIONAL HOCKEY LEAGUE (NHL) and are based in Anaheim, California. The Ducks won their only Stanley Cup in 2007.

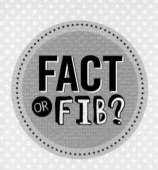

A football team must have at least seven players.

When playing **RACQUETBALL**, the server can hit any of the four walls.

A CHILD 7 TO 12 YEARS OLD NEEDS UP TO 11 HOURS OF SLEEP EACH NIGHT.

A football team needs a minimum of 7 players and a maximum of 11 players.

FIB

In racquetball, only THE FRONT WALL must be hit during a serve. The server will lose a turn if any of the other walls are hit.

FACT

IT IS RECOMMENDED THAT CHILDREN AGES 7 TO 12 GET 10 TO 11 HOURS OF SLEEP EACH NIGHT. YOUR BODY AND BRAIN WORK BETTER WITH THE RIGHT AMOUNT OF SLEEP.

FACT OR **FIB?**

THERE ARE 206 BONES IN THE HUMAN BODY.

Playing sports can help students do better in school.

OF THE 206 BONES IN THE HUMAN BODY, 25% ARE IN YOUR FEET! MANY OF THE BONES IN YOUR FEET ARE TEENY-TINY!

Studies have shown that the physical activity children get from sports helps improve memory and concentration, which helps them do better in school.

In 2012, a record **145 WATER SKIERS** were pulled behind a boat in Tasmania, Australia. To qualify for the record, they traveled for a full nautical mile without falling!

FIB

A Major League baseball has exactly 110 stitches.

DIFFERENT STATES HAVE DIFFERENT PERCENTAGES OF ACTIVE AND HEALTHY ADULTS.

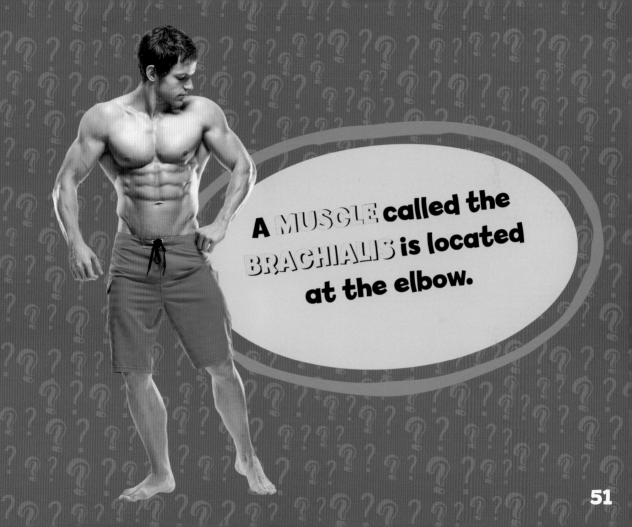

A **MUSCLE** called the **BRACHIALIS** is located at the elbow.

FIB

A regulation baseball used in the Major Leagues has exactly **108 DOUBLE STITCHES**. The components are made in the United States, then shipped to Costa Rica, where it takes about 15 minutes to assemble and stitch each ball.

FACT

THE STATE WITH THE MOST ACTIVE ADULTS IS VERMONT, WITH 65.3% OF THE POPULATION EXERCISING 3 TIMES A WEEK FOR AT LEAST 30 MINUTES. VERMONT IS FOLLOWED BY HAWAII AT 62.2% AND MONTANA AT 60.1%. AN AVERAGE STATE WILL HAVE 51.6% OF ITS POPULATION EXERCISING REGULARLY.

The **BRACHIALIS MUSCLE** helps your upper arm muscles bend at the **ELBOW** and move your lower arm up or down. You use this muscle when you hit a tennis ball or swing a baseball bat.

53

FACT OR FIB?

"Tennis leg" is a pain in the upper

THIGH MUSCLES.

The game of **LACROSSE** was invented by **NATIVE AMERICAN** tribes.

MOST AMERICAN CHILDREN SPEND 7 1/2 HOURS PER DAY IN FRONT OF A SCREEN.

Tennis leg is a **SWELLING** or or **WEAKENING** of the back of the **LOWER LEG**, starting at the the back of the knee. It can be caused by the repetitive movements of reaching for the tennis ball.

The original rules of **LACROSSE** are unknown, but rules were officially set up in 1794 during a game between the **SENECA** and **MOHAWK NATIONS**.

FACT

FACT

THE 7 1/2 HOURS AN AVERAGE CHILD SPENDS IN FRONT OF A SCREEN EACH DAY INCLUDE WATCHING TELEVISION, USING A COMPUTER, AND PLAYING VIDEO GAMES. SCIENTISTS HAVE LINKED TOO MUCH SITTING TO AN INCREASE IN MANY DISEASES, INCLUDING HEART DISEASE AND SOME CANCERS.

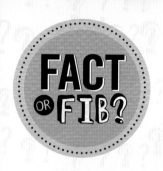
FACT OR FIB?

EATING **ALMONDS** CAN MAKE YOUR HAIR GROW FASTER.

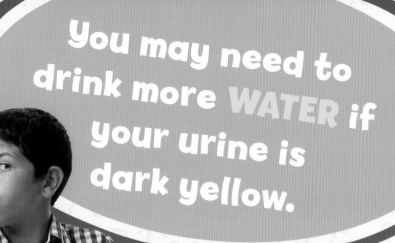

You may need to drink more WATER if your urine is dark yellow.

At the first modern OLYMPICS, third-place winners did not receive medals.

59

ALMONDS DO NOT MAKE YOUR HAIR GROW FASTER, BUT THEY DO CONTAIN A SUBSTANCE CALLED PHOSPHORUS, WHICH HELPS BUILD STRONG BONES AND TEETH.

FIB

FACT

Dehydration is when your body doesn't have enough WATER to work correctly. You can become dehydrated after sweating or when you are tired or sick. Normal urine should be PALE YELLOW so you know you are not dehydrated.

FACT

First-place winners at the 1896 Olympics in Athens, Greece, received SILVER MEDALS and OLIVE BRANCHES, and second-place finishers received laurel branches and bronze medals. The modern gold, silver, and bronze medals started in 1904 at the St. Louis Olympics.

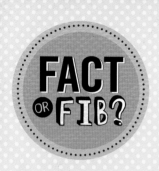

FACT OR **FIB?**

Running burns at least 10 calories per minute.

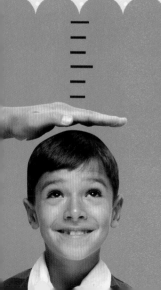

Children grow at a rate of about ONE INCH (2.5 cm) PER YEAR.

BROCCOLI HAS TWICE AS MUCH VITAMIN C AS AN ORANGE.

FACT

Even the slowest jogger can burn at least 10 calories per minute hitting the road or the treadmill. The faster you run, the more calories you burn per minute.

FIB

Children grow about 2½ **INCHES** (6.4 cm) each year until they are teens. At that point they may grow **UP TO 4 INCHES** (10.2 cm) per year until they reach adult height.

FACT

ALTHOUGH ORANGES ARE KNOWN FOR THEIR HIGH LEVELS OF VITAMIN C, THE SAME SERVING SIZE OF BROCCOLI HAS DOUBLE THE AMOUNT OF VITAMIN C!

ABOUT 500 MILLION PAIRS OF RUNNING SHOES ARE SOLD AROUND THE WORLD EACH YEAR.

Eating junk food can lead to diseases such as diabetes and depression.

FIB

A LOT MORE THAN 500 MILLION PAIRS OF RUNNING SHOES ARE SOLD AROUND THE WORLD EACH YEAR. THE ACTUAL FIGURE IS OVER 1 BILLION PAIRS!

FACT

Processed sugars found in junk foods and sodas raise the body's insulin levels, which can lead to diabetes. Trans fats and saturated fats found in junk food raise the risk for depression by 58%.

FACT

The sport of **CURLING** requires skill and strategy to slide the "stones" to the right place. Much like the game of chess, there is some **REAL THINKING** involved.

The **BOSTON RED SOX** won the first World Series in 1903.

BABIES ARE BORN WITH MORE BONES THAN ADULTS.

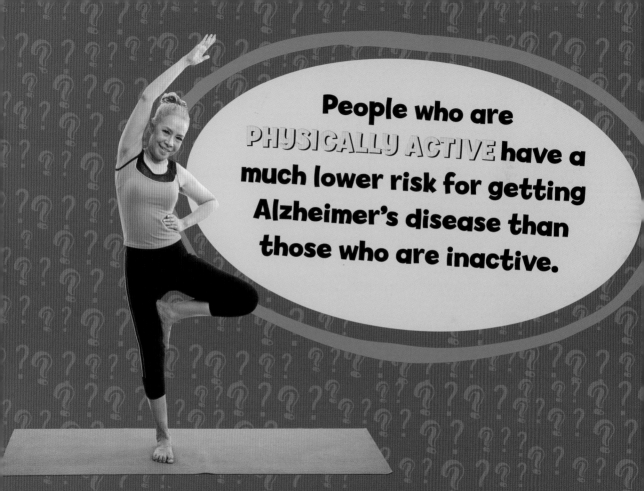

People who are PHYSICALLY ACTIVE have a much lower risk for getting Alzheimer's disease than those who are inactive.

FIB

The **BOSTON AMERICANS** beat the Pittsburgh Pirates five games to three in the first World Series championship in 1903. The team did not become the Boston Red Sox until 1907.

BABIES HAVE OVER 300 BONES, BUT AS THE BODY GROWS, SOME BONES FUSE TOGETHER. ADULTS HAVE A TOTAL OF 206 BONES.

FACT

A study from Sweden found a 60% LOWER RISK for Alzheimer's disease among ACTIVE PEOPLE compared to inactive people.

FACT

The human body replaces the lining of its stomach every **THREE TO FIVE DAYS.**

RACEHORSES can wear out their **HORSESHOES** in a single race.

THE PRODUCTION OF ONE MEDAL FROM THE 2014 SOCHI OLYMPICS TOOK 5 HOURS TO MAKE.

FACT

Stomach acids would break through the lining if it did not replace itself frequently. Stomach acids have to be **STRONG** to help break down and digest food.

Some **RACEHORSES** need to have their shoes replaced after **EACH RACE** or group of races because they wear them out so **QUICKLY**.

FACT

FIB

EACH MEDAL FROM THE 2014 SOCHI OLYMPICS TOOK AN AVERAGE OF **18 HOURS** TO CRAFT AND PRODUCE BECAUSE OF THE DETAILED DESIGN. THE SOCHI MEDAL IS ALSO ONE OF THE **LARGEST** TO BE GIVEN OUT AT OLYMPIC GAMES. THE GOLD MEDAL IS 3.9 INCHES (9.9 CM) ACROSS.

FACT OR **FIB?**

Baseball legend Babe Ruth wore a cabbage leaf under his cap to keep cool.

HUMAN FEET HAVE
500,000
SWEAT GLANDS.

The **WORLD CUP** soccer tournament is held **EVERY YEAR** at a different location around the world.

FACT

Nicknamed the Bambino and the Sultan of Swat, Babe Ruth replaced the cabbage leaf under his cap every two innings so that it was fresh and cool.

FACT

HUMAN FEET CAN MAKE MORE THAN A PINT OF SWEAT EVERY DAY FROM THEIR 500,000 SWEAT GLANDS. THEY CAN GIVE OFF A PRETTY BAD ODOR!

The **WORLD CUP** is a soccer tournament held every **4 YEARS.** Teams from different countries face off against one another at a chosen location.

FIB

FACT OR **FIB?**

Football, soccer, and rugby were all developed from the same sport.

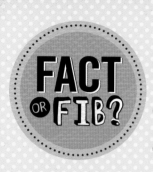

During a lifetime, the average person can fill TWO SWIMMING POOLS with SALIVA.

BOTH OF YOUR LUNGS ARE EXACTLY THE SAME SIZE.

In the **1800s**, variations of **soccer, rugby,** and the game we now know as **football** were played among schoolchildren in England. The games later branched off and developed their own rules.

The mouth produces about **25,000** quarts (23,658 L) of **SALIVA** during a lifetime to help break down food and make chewing and swallowing easier.

FIB YOUR LEFT LUNG IS A TINY BIT SMALLER THAN YOUR RIGHT LUNG. THAT'S BECAUSE 2/3 OF YOUR HEART IS ON THE LEFT SIDE OF THE BODY AND TAKES UP SOME EXTRA SPACE.

FACT or FIB?

THE WORD GYMNASIUM LITERALLY MEANS "TO EXERCISE NAKED."

During the course of a **SOCCER GAME**, a player may run more than **10 MILES** (16 km).

There is enough iron in your body to make a 3-inch nail.

FACT

THE WORD GYMNASIUM COMES FROM THE GREEK WORD GYMNAZEIN, WHICH MEANS "TO EXERCISE NAKED." ANCIENT GREEKS EXERCISED NAKED IN PUBLIC GYMS TO HONOR BOTH THE HUMAN FORM AND THE GODS THAT CREATED IT. TODAY GYMNASIUMS ARE STILL A PLACE TO EXERCISE, BUT WITH CLOTHING ON!

Soccer players don't quite run a whole 10 miles (16 km), but they often run **MORE THAN 6 MILES** (10 km) during a game. That's like a marathon every four games!

FIB

FACT

Iron is a natural substance in the body. We get it from eating foods such as meats and fish. Some vegetables, such as spinach and broccoli, also have iron.

A pound of fat is about 4,500 calories.

OVER THE COURSE OF A DAY, YOU BECOME .39 INCHES (1 CM) SHORTER.

One MARATHON RUNNER set a record by running a marathon each day for 365 CONSECUTIVE DAYS.

A pound of fat is about **3,500 CALORIES**. To burn one pound from your body, you must burn **3,500 MORE** calories than you eat.

FIB

FACT

THE STANDING AND MOVING YOU DO DURING EACH DAY PRESSES THE MATERIALS BETWEEN YOUR BONES TOGETHER A TINY BIT. THE BODY RETURNS TO NORMAL WHEN YOU SLEEP.

Nicknamed the "MARATHON MAN," Stefaan Engels from Belgium set the 365-day marathon record in 2011 at age 49.

FACT

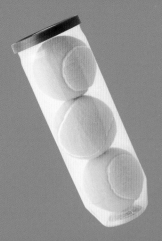

During the WIMBLEDON CHAMPIONSHIP games, 4,200 tennis balls are used.

A WORLD CUP TROPHY WAS STOLEN IN LONDON, ENGLAND, AND FOUND SEVERAL DAYS LATER BY A DOG.

FACT

The body burns anywhere between **50 AND 90 CALORIES** per hour while sleeping and watching television. But at least you're less likely to **SNACK IN YOUR SLEEP!**

FIB The world-famous Wimbledon Championships have about **660 TENNIS MATCHES**, which require about **54,250 TENNIS BALLS**!

FACT

IN 1966, THIEVES ABANDONED A STOLEN WORLD CUP TROPHY, WHICH WAS FOUND BY A DOG NAMED PICKLES WHILE OUT WALKING WITH ITS OWNER. THE SAME TROPHY WAS STOLEN AGAIN IN 1983 BUT NEVER RECOVERED.

Spicy peppers
have major
health benefits.

A baseball game
is actually
18 MINUTES LONG.

EATING **BREAKFAST** CAN HELP A PERSON LOSE WEIGHT.

Chili peppers offer lots of vitamin C. Peppers have two and a half times more vitamin C than oranges.

When you count only the time the ball is in play, a baseball game takes ABOUT 18 MINUTES, even though Major League games often run about 3 hours long.

SCIENTISTS ONCE THOUGHT THAT **EATING BREAKFAST** HELPED PEOPLE EAT LESS DURING THE DAY. BUT NEW RESEARCH SHOWS THAT EATING BREAKFAST HAS NO IMPACT ON HOW MANY CALORIES ARE EATEN OVERALL IN A DAY.

FIB

FACT OR FIB?

When a food label says "natural ingredients," it could mean crushed bugs.

Major League baseballs are SMEARED WITH MUD to remove the slick factory coating.

KITE FLYING IS
A PROFESSIONAL SPORT
IN THE UNITED STATES.

FACT A red food dye called "**carmine**" is made of crushed cochineal **insects**, which gives food a rich red color. To produce a pound of the dye, about 70,000 insects are needed.

So that pitchers can get a better **FACT** grip on a new baseball, each one is carefully covered in a light coating of **MUD** taken from the shores of the **DELAWARE RIVER**.

FIB

IN SEVERAL ASIAN COUNTRIES, INCLUDING THAILAND **AND INDIA,** KITE FLYING IS A PROFESSIONAL SPORT.

FOOTBALL GAMES ARE DIVIDED INTO FOUR QUARTERS, EACH ONE A HALF HOUR LONG.

Baseball UMPIRES used to sit in padded rocking chairs during games.

People who eat PIZZA regularly are less likely to develop some forms of cancer.

107

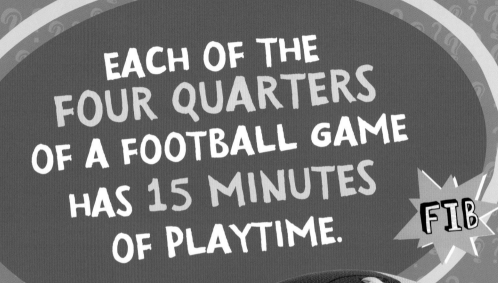

EACH OF THE
FOUR QUARTERS
OF A FOOTBALL GAME
HAS 15 MINUTES
OF PLAYTIME.

FIB

FACT

Before 1859, UMPIRES sat in padded rocking chairs behind the catcher. Their position was a little too comfortable, and it was not the best place to get a good view of everything on the field!

FACT

A study showed that pizza eaters are less likely to get cancers of the mouth, colon, and esophagus. Pizza sauce is high in lycopene, an antioxidant found in tomatoes that has been known to help prevent cancer.

FACT OR FIB?

A football field is **120 YARDS** (109.7 m) long.

The football playing field is **100 YARDS** (91.4 m) long, plus there are **10-YARD** (9.1-m) end zones on each side. The field is **53 YARDS** (48.5 m) wide.

FACT

FIB

THE BRAIN STOPS GROWING IN SIZE AT ABOUT AGE 18. HOWEVER, YOU CAN KEEP LEARNING THROUGHOUT YOUR WHOLE LIFE.

FACT

Our brains get DISTRACTED BY MUSIC, so it's easier to KEEP WORKING OUT when we're listening to songs we like.

Lacrosse has the **SAME** set of **RULES** for everyone who plays.

There are over 640 MUSCLES in the human body.

IN BOWLING, THREE STRIKES IN A ROW IS CALLED A "TURKEY."

FIB

There are SEPARATE SETS of lacrosse rules for MEN, WOMEN, BOYS, and GIRLS.

FACT

Muscles make up the body's **MUSCULAR SYSTEM**, which includes muscles that move body parts inside and outside the body.

FACT

AROUND THANKSGIVING AND CHRISTMAS IN THE LATE 1800s, BOWLERS WERE REWARDED WITH A FREE TURKEY IF THEY BOWLED THREE STRIKES IN A ROW. THE ACCOMPLISHMENT IS ALSO KNOWN AS A "GOBBLER."

A **basketball game** is made of two teams, each with eight players.

The human heart beats about **35 MILLION** times per year.

BADMINTON BIRDIES USED IN OLYMPIC COMPETITIONS MUST HAVE EXACTLY 16 FEATHERS.

A basketball team is made of **five players**. Of those five players, there are two forwards, two guards, and one center.

FIB

Thirty-five million heartbeats per year is about **100,000 PER DAY**. That means your heart will beat 2.5 billion times during your lifetime.

FACT

FACT BY USING THE SAME KIND OF BIRDIE IN EVERY COMPETITION, PLAYERS AND JUDGES ARE SURE THAT THE GAME IS FAIR. THE BIRDIE IS THE SAME WEIGHT AND SIZE IN EACH COMPETITION.

FACT OR FIB?

About 8% of children suffer from some kind of food allergy.

Most scuba divers will go **150 FEET** (45.7 meters) underwater during a single dive.

THE HEART PUMPS ABOUT 1 MILLION BARRELS OF BLOOD DURING A LIFETIME.

Food allergies only strike about 2% of adults, but 8% of children suffer from some kind of food allergy. Some of the most common food allergies include sensitivities to nuts and seafood.

It is not recommended that a scuba diver go **BELOW 60 FEET** (18.3 meters) during a dive. The air pressure gets too high below that point, and it may take the diver too long to get back to the surface with his or her air supply.

FACT

DURING A PERSON'S LIFETIME, THE AMOUNT OF BLOOD THAT THE HEART PUMPS CAN FILL ONE MILLION BARRELS, OR THREE GIANT OIL TANKERS. THAT'S A LOT OF BLOOD FOR FOR ONE PERSON!

FACT OR FIB?

"GOOFY FOOT" IS A SURFING TERM.

Basketball was **INVENTED** by a **GYM TEACHER**.

Fats make up 10% of a healthy diet for a child.

"GOOFY FOOT" IS THE TERM USED FOR A SURFER WHO STANDS ON A SURFBOARD WITH HIS OR HER RIGHT FOOT IN FRONT. STANDING ON A SURFBOARD WITH THE LEFT FOOT LEADING IS CALLED A "REGULAR FOOT" STANCE.

FACT

In 1891, **JAMES NAISMITH** occupied students indoors during the winter by nailing peach baskets to the wall and having **STUDENTS** throw balls into them. Many of the original rules of his game are still used today.

FIB

A 10- to 11-year-old's diet should be made of 25% to 35% fat per day to help with brain development.

A touchdown in football is worth SEVEN POINTS.

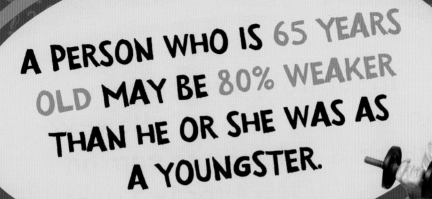

A PERSON WHO IS 65 YEARS OLD MAY BE 80% WEAKER THAN HE OR SHE WAS AS A YOUNGSTER.

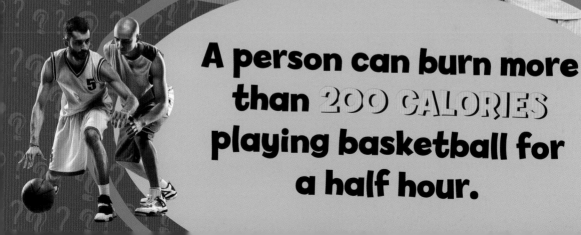

A person can burn more than 200 CALORIES playing basketball for a half hour.

In football, a touchdown is worth **SIX POINTS**. However, there is a chance to earn an **EXTRA POINT** or two right after the touchdown is scored.

FIB

FACT

SOMEONE WHO DOES NOT EXERCISE REGULARLY WILL LOSE MUSCLE TONE. OVER MANY YEARS THIS CAN LEAD TO A LOSS OF ABOUT 80 PERCENT OF A PERSON'S STRENGTH BY THE TIME HE OR SHE IS 65 YEARS OLD.

FACT

A 154-pound man who is 5 feet 10 inches tall can BURN 220 CALORIES during a vigorous game of basketball. That's about the same number of calories in an apple and a granola bar together.

FACT OR **FIB?**

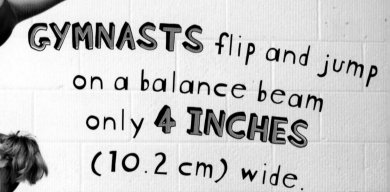

GYMNASTS flip and jump on a balance beam only **4 INCHES** (10.2 cm) wide.

Many sports require their REFEREES to be very PHYSICALLY FIT.

EXERCISING ON AN EMPTY STOMACH BURNS MORE FAT.

Balance beams are **4 INCHES (10.2 CM) WIDE, 16 FEET AND 5 INCHES (5 M) LONG,** and **4 FEET (1.2 M)** off the floor. They are covered in suede or leather to keep gymnasts from slipping.

FACT

FACT

The referees in a hockey game **MUST SKATE** up and down the ice rink throughout the **WHOLE GAME** to make sure the game is **FAIR**. Soccer and basketball referees run many miles each game.

EXERCISING ON AN EMPTY STOMACH WILL BURN MUSCLE INSTEAD OF FAT, AND THE BODY WILL BECOME WEAKER.

FIB

FACT OR **FIB?**

Tug-of-war was once an Olympic sport.

Doing many types of exercise can increase your chances of getting **INJURED**.

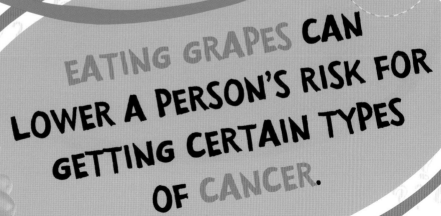

EATING GRAPES CAN LOWER A PERSON'S RISK FOR GETTING CERTAIN TYPES OF CANCER.

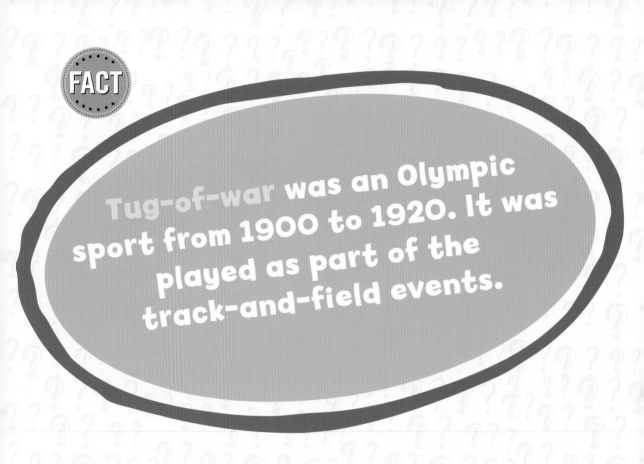

FACT

Tug-of-war was an Olympic sport from 1900 to 1920. It was played as part of the track-and-field events.

Doing different types of exercise can make you **LESS LIKELY** to become injured because you are strengthening different parts of your body.

FIB

FACT

GRAPES HAVE HIGH LEVELS OF ANTIOXIDANTS KNOWN FOR SLOWING OR PREVENTING MANY TYPES OF CANCER. THEY ALSO HELP PREVENT HEART DISEASE AND HIGH BLOOD PRESSURE.

There are **162 GAMES** in a regular baseball season.

About **25%** of people do not get enough **IRON** in their diets.

TENNIS BALLS ARE COVERED IN FELT TO MAKE THEM MOVE FASTER.

The baseball season is played from early April until the last week in September. Each team plays 162 games.

A lack of iron can cause a condition called ANEMIA, which makes you feel tired and look pale. Foods high in iron include spinach, beans, and meats.

FIB

THE FELT THAT COVERS TENNIS BALLS IS MEANT TO SLOW THE BALL DOWN SO THAT IT IS EASIER FOR PLAYERS TO CONTROL.

STRETCHING MAKES MUSCLES BIGGER AND STRONGER.

A can of soda contains about **10 TEASPOONS** of sugar.

The dimples on a golf ball make the ball fly farther when hit.

FACT

The **EXTRA SUGAR** in soft drinks makes it easy for people to **GAIN WEIGHT**. It also promotes tooth decay and other poor eating habits.

The dimples on the golf ball create less pull and drag as it flies through the air. This helps the ball go farther.

FACT

There is an OLYMPIC SPORT that requires athletes to LIE DOWN.

CANTALOUPE HELPS YOU HAVE GOOD VISION.

VITAMIN D is found in most healthy foods.

In the **LUGE COMPETITION**, athletes lie down on a sled and race on an icy, downhill track. They reach speeds of up to **90 MILES** (144.8 km) per hour!

FACT

FACT

CANTALOUPES ARE HIGH IN VITAMIN A, WHICH IS NEEDED FOR HEALTHY EYES AND VISION. VITAMIN A ALSO HELPS KEEP YOUR TEETH HEALTHY!

FIB

Some fish, such as tuna and salmon, have vitamin D. Other foods, such as milk, have it added. The BEST SOURCE of VITAMIN D is getting more natural SUNLIGHT.

WHOLE MILK

Milk

Milk

FACT OR FIB?

YOGA is a practice that is more than 5,000 YEARS OLD.

FRESH fruits and vegetables are **HEALTHIER** than frozen ones.

THERE IS A STRENGTH EXERCISE CALLED "THE DEAD BUG."

FACT

The **ORIGINAL YOGA** postures
may not look exactly like
the ones practiced today.
But the practice that connects mind
and body can be traced back to
INDIA and has been refined
over the centuries.

FIB

Frozen fruits and veggies are very nutritious. Seasonal, fresh produce is great, but FROZEN IS AVAILABLE ALL YEAR LONG!

·MIXED VEGETABLES·

THE DEAD BUG IS AN ABDOMINAL EXERCISE. TO TRY IT, LIE ON YOUR BACK AND LIFT YOUR RIGHT KNEE TOWARD YOUR CHEST AND YOUR LEFT ARM ABOVE YOUR HEAD. RETURN TO THE STARTING POSITION AND SWITCH SIDES.

FACT

A peanut is not really a **NUT**.

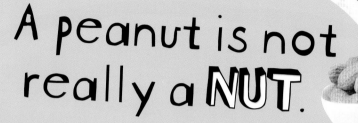

"ULTIMATE" IS A FRISBEE GAME SIMILAR TO GOLF.

FACT

A 2010 study by the Outdoor Foundation found that people who switch from driving to biking to work lost an average of 13 pounds (5.9 kg) in their first year of biking.

FACT

Walnuts, almonds, and pecans are all really nuts, but the peanut is not. A peanut comes from a type of plant called a legume.

FIB

"ULTIMATE" IS A FRISBEE GAME SIMILAR TO SOCCER OR BASKETBALL. IT IS PLAYED WITH TWO TEAMS THAT TRY TO SCORE A GOAL AGAINST THE OPPOSING TEAM.

FACT OR FIB?

Fruits and vegetables make people happier.

The more you SWEAT while working out, the more CALORIES you have burned.

THE **FASTEST TENNIS SERVE** BY A WOMAN WAS RECORDED AT ABOUT 131 MILES (210.8 KM) PER HOUR.

FACT

A study by New Zealand researchers found that an increase in fruits and vegetables in people's diets made them feel more creative, more curious, and happier. It was easier for them to complete simple tasks.

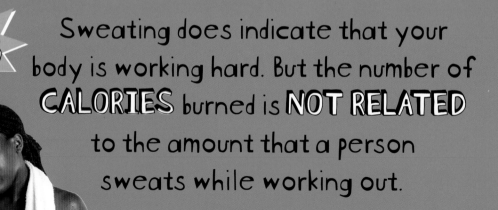

FIB

Sweating does indicate that your body is working hard. But the number of CALORIES burned is NOT RELATED to the amount that a person sweats while working out.

SABINE LISICKI SET THE RECORD FOR THE FASTEST SERVE BY A WOMAN IN 2014, BREAKING A RECORD HELD BY VENUS WILLIAMS.

FACT

FACT OR FIB?

A HIGH JUMPER IS DISQUALIFIED IF HE OR SHE FAILS TO MAKE IT OVER THE BAR SUCCESSFULLY THREE TIMES IN A ROW.

The **STRONGEST** muscle in the human body is the **HEART**.

Lemons are one of the healthiest foods.

FACT

DURING A HIGH-JUMP EVENT, THE BAR GETS RAISED HIGHER AND HIGHER. AFTER FAILING TO MAKE IT OVER THE BAR THREE TIMES IN A ROW, A HIGH JUMPER IS DISQUALIFIED.

The strongest muscle is the **JAW MUSCLE**, or chewer muscle, called the masseter. The human jaw can bite down with over 200 pounds (91 kg) of force.

FIB

A **lemon** is a superfood. Just one lemon contains almost half of the **vitamin C** you need in a day.

FACT

FACT OR **FIB?**

ROCK CLIMBING burns very few calories.

An adult can burn about **370 CALORIES** an hour rock climbing. The energy needed to reach and climb from rock to rock makes the sport quite difficult!

FIB

BOWLING IS THE SPORT THAT EARNS THE MOST MONEY FOR CHARITY. VARIOUS BOWLING FUND-RAISERS EARN MORE THAN $225 MILLION FOR CHARITY EACH YEAR.

FACT

FACT

UNICYCLE competitions take place all around the world. The best and fastest one-wheeled cyclers compete at an event called **UNICON** that takes place every two years.

AVOCADOS are considered unhealthy because they contain too much fat.

Tennis fans watching the Wimbledon Championships eat more than 30 TONS OF STRAWBERRIES during the event each year.

JUMPING ROPE WORKS OUT THE CALVES MORE THAN ANY OTHER MUSCLES.

AVOCADOS do contain a lot of fat—in fact they are 85% fat! But they contain monounsaturated fat, which is a **HEALTHY** type of fat that is good for your body.

FIB

FACT

During the tennis championships at WIMBLEDON, fans snack on strawberries. Each year, about 30.8 TONS (28 metric tons) of strawberries are ordered for the crowds.

IN ADDITION TO GIVING YOUR **HEART** A GREAT WORKOUT, JUMPING ROPE WORKS OUT THE BACKS OF THE LOWER LEGS, CALLED THE **CALVES.** IT ALSO WORKS OUT THE TOPS OF THE LEGS AND THE BUTT.

FACT

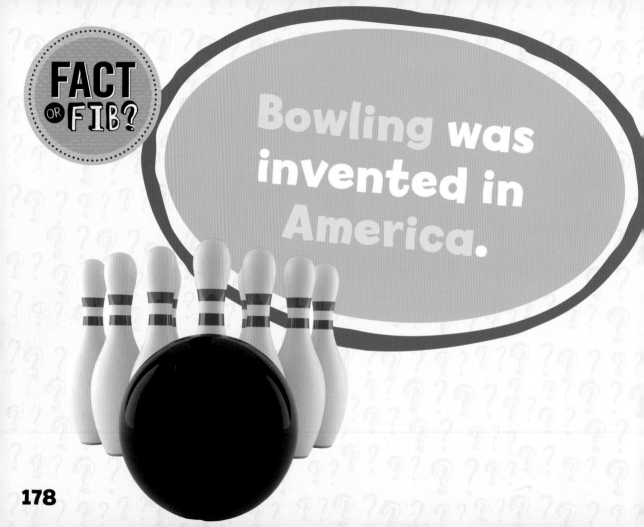

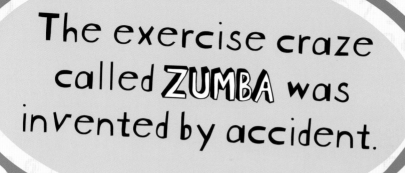

The exercise craze called **ZUMBA** was invented by accident.

CUB SCOUTS CAN PLAY "ULTIMATE" TO EARN FITNESS AND PARTICIPATION AWARDS.

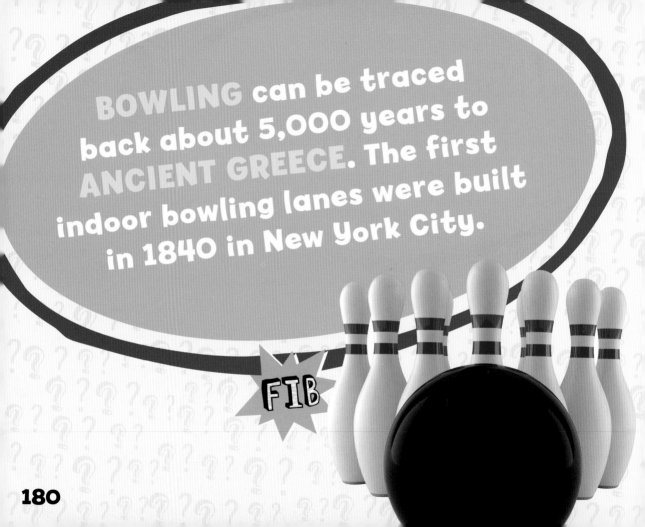

BOWLING can be traced back about 5,000 years to ANCIENT GREECE. The first indoor bowling lanes were built in 1840 in New York City.

FIB

180

FACT

ZUMBA was invented in the **1990s** when a fitness instructor forgot to bring the right music to his aerobics class. He used the **SALSA** and **MERENGUE** tapes he had with him and started a new exercise trend.

FACT

ULTIMATE FRISBEE IS ONE OF MANY CATEGORIES IN WHICH A CUB SCOUT CAN EARN AN **AWARD**. THERE ARE ALSO AWARDS FOR OTHER SPORTS, ACADEMIC SUBJECTS, AND ACTIVITIES.

FACT OR FIB?

All professional sports teams in **Pittsburgh** wear **black-and-gold uniforms.**

Scientists think that DARK CHOCOLATE can improve your exercise performance.

THE **MUSCLES** THAT FOCUS YOUR **EYES** MOVE ABOUT 1,000 TIMES PER DAY.

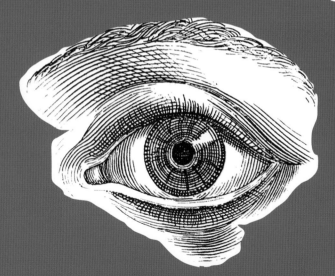

Pittsburgh, Pennsylvania, is the **only city** in which all of its **major sports** teams—baseball, hockey, and football—wear black and gold.

FACT

FACT

Studies of MICE have shown that feeding them the key ingredient in dark chocolate for two weeks made them able to EXERCISE LONGER and improved their muscles.

THE EYE MUSCLES MOVE ABOUT 100,000 TIMES PER DAY TO FOCUS AND KEEP YOUR VISION SHARP. YOU WOULD HAVE TO WALK 50 MILES (80.5 KM) TO GIVE YOUR LEGS THE SAME WORKOUT.

FACT OR FIB?

BIKING IS BIG IN CHINA, WITH MORE THAN A HALF BILLION BICYCLES IN THE COUNTRY.

Most mail carriers walk about **4 MILES** (6.4 km) per day.

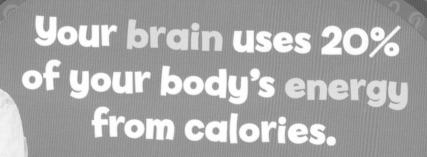

Your brain uses 20% of your body's energy from calories.

FACT

THE BICYCLE WAS INTRODUCED IN CHINA IN THE LATE 1800s AND IS NOW A VERY POPULAR WAY TO GET AROUND. THE CHINESE GOVERNMENT HAS INTRODUCED BIKE-SHARING PROGRAMS IN CITIES TO REDUCE TRAFFIC AND POLLUTION.

Most mail carriers walk about
8 MILES (12.9 km) per day!
Janitors walk about 5 miles (8 km)
and restaurant workers walk
about 4 miles (6.4 km) per day.

FIB

In addition to using 20%
of the body's calories, the
brain also uses 20% of the
body's oxygen.

FACT

The **FIVE RINGS** on the Olympic flag represent parts of the world.

THE **SLOWEST SWIMMING** STROKE IN COMPETITION IS THE **BREASTSTROKE**.

Blood takes an HOUR to move around an adult human body.

The yellow, green, red, black, and blue interlocking rings represent the FIVE main areas of the WORLD that compete in the international games: the Americas, Asia, Australia, Europe, and Africa.

THE BREASTSTROKE IS THE SLOWEST STROKE. THE MOVEMENTS CAUSE MORE DRAG OF WATER AGAINST THE BODY, SO IT TAKES LONGER FOR BREASTSTROKE COMPETITORS TO FINISH A RACE THAN IF THEY WERE DOING ANOTHER STROKE. THE FREESTYLE STROKE IS THE FASTEST.

FACT

Blood takes only about a MINUTE to move around an adult human body. Each HEARTBEAT pumps out about 2.4 ounces (71 ml).

FIB

Americans will drink about **12,000 GALLONS (45,425 L)** of liquid in their lifetime.

The average **BASEBALL** in a major league game is used for about **5 to 7 GAMES.**

BASKETBALL BECAME PART OF THE OLYMPIC GAMES IN 1936.

FACT

Not only will each American drink **12,000 GALLONS** (45,425 L) of liquid in his or her lifetime, each will also eat about **50 TONS** (45.4 metric tons) of food!

NEW BASEBALLS are used for **EACH GAME**, and the average ball is used for only five to seven pitches. Many are lost in the stands, and scuffed balls are used for batting practice.

THE FIRST OLYMPIC BASKETBALL GAMES WERE PLAYED AS PART OF THE SUMMER GAMES IN BERLIN, GERMANY, IN 1936.

OR FIB?

RABADZHIEVA 5

FILIPOVA M. 13

The world's longest volleyball game lasted 85 HOURS.

FACT

The longest volleyball game was started on December 27, 2011, between two teams from the Netherlands. It ended three days later!

With **116** lanes, the Inazawa Grand Bowling Center holds the Guinness World Record for the **LARGEST BOWLING ALLEY** in the world.

FACT

FIB

THE HUMAN BODY IS 50% TO **75% WATER.** MEN ARE USUALLY MADE OF MORE WATER THAN WOMEN.

INDEX

NOTE: Page numbers in parentheses indicate FACT or FIB answers.

203

Alamy
© Itar-Tass Photo Agency: 95 right; © Reda & Co srl: 150: © Jack Sullivan: 10 right, 12; © Gerry Yardy: 59 bottom

Corbis
© Michael Interisano/Design Pics: 39 left

Getty Images
82 top; © Paolo Bruno: 198; © Chris Clinton: 31, 33; © Dorling Kindersley: 42 bottom, 44; © Dwight Eschliman: 62 bottom, 64; © Lluis Gene/AFP: 91; © Thearon W. Henderson: 182 top; © Matthew Holt/Visuals Unlimited, Inc: 111 right, 113; © Peter Macdiarmid: 34, 36; © Brad Mangin: 142 top; © John Tlumacki/ The Boston Globe: 14; © Jung Yeon-Je/ AFP: 67

iStockphoto
© 4x6: 22 bottom, 24, 114, 116; © alex-mit: 83, 85; © anna1311: 7 left; © 187 bottom; © Matthew Benoit: 50 right, 52, 102 bottom; © Jill Chen: 142 bottom; © chictype: 66 left, 68; © cjp: 35 right; © cris180: 159 left; © C-You: 18 left, 20; © doram: 50 left; © Eugene_ Onischenko: 131 left; © William Fawcett: 186; © fcafotodigital: 90 right, 92; © Christopher Futcher: 127 top; © gemena communication: 158; © GlobalStock: 131 right; © hddigital: 123; © bonnie Jacobs: 118 bottom; © Aleksander Kaczmarek: 18 right; © kcline: 26, 28; © Issam Khriji: 46 top; © mysondanube: 23; © nickp37: 118 top, 121; © OJO Images: 94; © Tabitha

Patrick: 134; © pixdeluxe: 111 left; © Andrey Popov: 27 right; © Prebranac: 90 left; © Thomas Quack: 22 top; © ranplett: 98 left; © Andrew Rich: 110; © Lee Rogers: 99, 101; © RonOrmanJr: 171 left; © Charles Schmidt: 7 right, 9; © skynesher: 19; © Siri Stafford: 187 top, 189; © Talaj: 178, 180; © tilo: 115 right; © Vasiliki Varvaki: 63; © woraput: 71

Library of Congress
30 top

Newscom
© Reuters: 75 right, 77

Shutterstock
© adike: 167 top, 169; © AGIF: 79, 81; © Ahturner: 139 right, 141; © AlinaMD: 35 left; © American Spirit: 38, 40; © andersphoto: 87 left; © Anteromite: 183, 185; © Diego Barbieri: 82 bottom; © bikeriderlondon: 54, 56, 86; © Paolo Bona: 191 top; © Brocreative: 42 top; © Celig: 59 top; © Zdenka Darula: 179 top; © decade3d: 10 left; © EpicStockMedia: 126; © Greg Epperson: 170, 172; © Flashon Studio: 35 right, 137; © Mike Flippo: 46 bottom; © B. Franklin: 171 right; © Bill Frische: 55 left; © GlebStock: 78 left; © Rob Hainer: 179 bottom; © HitToon.Com: 122 top; © ITALO: 51; © jordache: 15 right; © MidoSemsem: 127 bottom, 129; © Cindy Minear: 39 right; © Natykach Nataliia: 74; © nathanmcc: 47, 49; © Natikka: 139 left; © Natursports: 166; © Kim Nguyen: 151

right; © Nomad_Soul: 199 right; © Olha Insight: 190; © OPgrapher: 30 bottom; © parinyabinsuk: 43; © Cheryl Ann Quigley: 75 left; © samsonovs: 182 bottom; © Sean Locke Photography: 70 top, 72, 107 right; © Serega K Photo & Video: 62 top; © Shooter Bob Square Lenses: 35 left; © Ljupco Smokovski: 15 left, 17, 87 right, 89; © tacar: 11; © T-Design: 163; © Dan Thornberg: 27 left; © wavebreakmedia: 138; © yanugkelid: 6

Thinkstock
130, 132; © Helder Almeida: 162 bottom, 164; © Mariusz Blach: 174, 176; © Comstock: 119; © Diane Diederich: 151 left, 153; © epantha: 155 right; © Yiap See Fat: 95 left, 97; © Fuse: 102 top; © Gewoldi: 70 bottom; © Gizelka: 143, 145; © Viktor Gladkov: 154; © Danny Hooks: 107 left; © Hyrma: 199 left, 201; © iSailorr: 147 bottom; © juefraphoto: 98 right; © Evgeny Karandaev: 194; © koosen: 195 right; © korionov: 191 bottom, 193; © leonello: 115 left; © Oleksiy Mark: 147 top; © m-ikeda: 195 left, 197; © miwa_in_oz: 58, 60; © monticelllo: 78 right; © Nagy-Bagoly Ilona: 162 top; © PhotoObjects.net: 122 bottom, 124, 155 left, 157; © Ridofranz: 146, 148; © Samohin: 167 bottom; © SerrNovik: 103, 105; © stanfram: 55 right; © Yuliyan Velchev: 159 right, 161; © Willard: 106, 108; © yalcinsonat1: 66 right, © zjzpp163: 175 right

We hope you enjoyed all the fun facts (and fibs!) about sports, fitness, and health. Check our other **FACT** OR **FIB?** books to test your knowledge of a range of subjects from dinosaurs to the human body to space and more!